I0019025

Trapped in the Digital Age:

The Silent Epidemic of Stress, Burnout, and Mental Exhaustion

How Your Phone Screen and Sedentary Life Are Rewiring Your Brain—And What We Must Do Before It's Too Late

By

Jack Michael

Jack Michael

Copyright © 2025 Jack Michael

All rights reserved.

DEDICATION

To everyone who has ever felt the weight of exhaustion pressing down, who has questioned why they feel drained even after a full night's sleep, and who wonders if life was always meant to be this overwhelming.

This book is for those fighting silent battles with stress, burnout, and digital fatigue—often unnoticed, but deeply felt.

May you find clarity, balance, and the courage to reclaim your peace. You deserve a life free from exhaustion. You deserve to breathe again.

Jack Michael

ACKNOWLEDGMENTS

This book would not have been possible without the countless conversations, research, and personal experiences that shaped its pages.

I am grateful to the experts, psychologists, and thought leaders whose work provided insight into the complexities of stress and burnout. To my family and friends—thank you for your unwavering support and understanding.

And to my readers, who seek change and balance in an overstimulated world—this book is for you. Your journey starts now.

Jack Michael

TABLE OF CONTENTS

INTRODUCTION

There was a time when silence existed. A time when the first moments of the morning were filled with nothing but the sound of birds outside the window or the rhythmic breath of waking up slowly, without urgency. Those days are gone. Now, before the second eye even opens, fingers are already reaching for a phone screen, scrolling through an avalanche of notifications, emails, and news alerts. The brain, still heavy from sleep, is jolted awake—not naturally, but through a forced, artificial stimulant. This is modern life, and it's killing us.

The world has never been more advanced, more connected, or more efficient. And yet, something is deeply wrong. Stress levels have skyrocketed to unprecedented levels. Burnout is no longer a problem exclusive to the overworked executive—students, parents, young professionals, even teenagers are experiencing symptoms of exhaustion that past generations might never have understood. The human brain, which evolved over thousands of years to survive in an environment of physical movement, natural light, and social bonds, is now trapped inside a digital box, overstimulated, overworked, and unable to rest.

Look around, and you'll see the signs everywhere. People moving through life in a haze, their faces buried in screens, their minds elsewhere, their bodies seated for hours on end. Anxiety has become the background noise of existence. Sleep disorders, fatigue, irritability—these aren't anomalies anymore; they are the norm. Work never really ends, because the office has been replaced by a pocket-sized device that never stops buzzing. Even relaxation is an illusion. Streaming a show, checking social media, mindlessly scrolling—none of it actually allows the brain to reset. Instead, it keeps it wired, constantly processing, never unplugging.

The most disturbing part? Most people don't even realize what's happening to them. The modern lifestyle has reprogrammed the brain in ways we don't fully understand, and the consequences are only beginning to surface. Burnout isn't just about feeling tired. Chronic stress isn't just about feeling overwhelmed. These are biological changes—real, physical transformations happening inside the body and mind. The neural pathways that once allowed for focus, patience, and deep thinking are being overwritten by a different kind of mental wiring: one that thrives on rapid consumption, short attention spans, and instant gratification.

This isn't alarmism. This isn't exaggeration. It's science. Studies have shown that the human brain is now being conditioned in ways that mimic addiction. The average person picks up their phone over 2,600 times a day. People spend hours scrolling, even when they don't want to. Sleep deprivation is at an all-time high. Work-life balance is collapsing. And yet, instead of recognizing these signs for what they are—a crisis—we continue to push forward, believing that exhaustion is just a part of modern existence.

But it doesn't have to be this way.

The problem isn't technology itself. The problem is how we've allowed it to consume us. The way we engage with screens, the way we let work seep into every hour of our lives, the way we sit for endless stretches of time without moving—these are the habits that are reshaping our bodies and minds. And the consequences won't just be mental fatigue or irritability. This crisis is leading to serious long-term damage: increased risks of anxiety disorders, depression, cognitive decline, even chronic physical illnesses. The cost of living like this isn't just a few bad nights of sleep or a little stress—it's the slow erosion of mental and physical well-being.

But here's the good news: once you **see** the problem for what it is, you can start reclaiming control. The same brain that has been rewired by digital addiction can also be rewired for balance, focus, and peace. The same body that has been trapped in a sedentary lifestyle can be reawakened. The same stress that has controlled you can be dismantled, if you understand its roots.

This book is not about telling you to quit your job, throw away your phone, or move to the mountains. It's about giving you the **knowledge** to understand what is happening to you—and the tools to fight back. It's about recognizing the patterns that have been designed to keep you exhausted and learning how to break them. It's about discovering how small, deliberate changes can restore clarity, energy, and control over your own mind.

You don't have to keep living this way. You don't have to accept burnout, mental fog, and stress as inevitable. The world may have changed, but you still have the power to choose how you interact with it.

You still have the ability to reset your brain, reclaim your focus, and rebuild the balance that modern life has stripped away.

If you're tired of feeling overwhelmed, if you've ever questioned why you can't seem to focus like you used to, if you're wondering why exhaustion feels permanent—keep reading. This book is your wake-up call. And once you see the truth, you'll never look at your screen, your stress, or your daily habits the same way again.

CHAPTER 1

The Science of Stress—Understanding the Invisible Burden

Stress is one of the most overused and least understood words in modern life. It's thrown around in casual conversations—*I'm so stressed about this deadline. That traffic was stressful. This week has been exhausting.* But what is stress, really? Beneath the surface of these everyday complaints lies a biological process that has been evolving for millions of years, designed to keep humans alive. The problem is that this system, perfected for survival in a prehistoric world, is now being hijacked by modern life in ways it was never meant to handle.

In its simplest form, stress is the body's response to a demand or challenge. It is not inherently bad. In fact, short bursts of stress, known as acute stress, are essential for survival. This is the kind of stress that sharpens focus before a big presentation, fuels motivation before an important task, or helps someone slam on the brakes in a split second to avoid an accident. The human body was built to handle these brief episodes of high alert, allowing for quick reactions and heightened awareness. Once the challenge passes, the body is supposed to return to a state of balance.

But that's **not** what's happening today.

Modern stress is no longer an occasional burst of adrenaline triggered by a life-threatening event. It has transformed into something relentless—**chronic stress**—a slow, continuous strain that never fully switches off. Unlike our ancestors, who faced stress in the form of an occasional wild animal or sudden danger, people today live in a world of **constant triggers**. Emails, notifications, deadlines, financial worries, social pressures—every minute brings another potential stressor. The problem is that the brain doesn't differentiate between a real physical threat and an overwhelming inbox. To the nervous system, an angry email from a boss can trigger the same **fight-or-flight** response that our ancestors experienced when encountering a predator.

This response is governed by a part of the brain called the **amygdala**, a tiny almond-shaped structure responsible for detecting threats. The moment stress is perceived, the amygdala sends an emergency signal, flooding the body with stress hormones—adrenaline and cortisol—designed to prepare for action. The heart races, blood pressure rises, muscles tense, and digestion slows, all to ensure maximum efficiency for either fighting or fleeing. This is what kept early humans alive in dangerous environments.

But in today's world, there's no tiger to outrun. There's just **more work, more notifications, and more mental clutter**. The stress response, meant to be short-lived, now runs on an endless loop. The body stays in a prolonged state of alert, unable to fully relax, and over time, this takes a **massive** toll.

Chronic stress isn't just an inconvenience—it **rewires the brain**. The prefrontal cortex, responsible for logic, planning, and self-control, begins to **shrink**, making it harder to concentrate or make rational decisions. At the same time, the amygdala, the brain's emotional center, grows **more reactive**, making everything feel **more overwhelming than it should**. This is why someone under constant stress can feel irritated by the smallest inconveniences or struggle with decisions that once felt effortless.

The effects don't stop at the brain. The body also suffers. **Prolonged exposure to stress hormones weakens the immune system, disrupts sleep, and**

increases the risk of heart disease, digestive issues, and mental health conditions like anxiety and depression. It explains why so many people today feel tired even after a full night's sleep or why stress-related illnesses like high blood pressure and migraines are on the rise. The modern body, like the modern brain, is trapped in a cycle of stress it wasn't designed to endure.

One of the most insidious aspects of chronic stress is **delayed stress reactions**—a phenomenon that explains why people often break down *after* a stressful period has ended. Soldiers returning from war, professionals finishing high-stakes projects, or even students after exams—they all seem fine in the moment, but once the immediate challenge is over, the body **collapses under the weight of everything it held together**. This explains why many people feel exhausted, irritable, or emotionally drained months after a major life event, as if their nervous system is only now processing the stress they ignored before.

The workplace has become **a breeding ground for stress**, and no industry is immune. It doesn't matter whether someone is an entry-level worker or a CEO—the pressure to perform, meet deadlines, and stay ahead in an ever-demanding job market is relentless. **Burnout** has become a **global epidemic**, affecting young professionals, parents juggling work and home life, and even students who are experiencing workplace-level stress before they've even entered the workforce.

Technology has only made it worse. The **inability to disconnect from work**—checking emails late at night, taking calls during vacations, feeling the constant pull to stay online—has blurred the boundaries between professional and personal life. Studies have shown that **60% of people experiencing burnout report an inability to "switch off" from work.** This perpetual connection keeps the stress response **active** at all times, making true relaxation nearly impossible.

Even those who don't work traditional jobs aren't exempt. The pressure to stay **visible, relevant, and engaged** in the digital world has created new forms of stress, from social comparison on social media to the feeling of always needing to respond, update, or be "on." What used to be **free time** is now filled with micro-stressors—responding to messages, keeping up with notifications, and scrolling through news that fuels even more anxiety.

This is the **silent burden** of modern life. It's invisible, creeping in slowly, reshaping thoughts, emotions, and health **without most people even realizing it**. It has become so **normalized** that many people don't even question why they feel exhausted, anxious, or mentally foggy. They assume it's just how life is now.

But understanding stress—what it is, how it works, and how it has been **manipulated** by the demands of the modern world—is the first step in breaking free from its grip. Because stress, left unchecked, doesn't just affect the present. It shapes the future. It determines **how long a person will live, how well they will age, and whether they will thrive or simply survive** in the years to come.

CHAPTER 2

Burnout—The New Global Pandemic

Burnout doesn't happen overnight. It's not like a car that suddenly stops working—it's more like an engine that has been running too hot for too long, gradually breaking down in ways that aren't obvious at first. By the time someone realizes they are burned out, they're often too deep into exhaustion to easily pull themselves out.

For years, burnout was misunderstood, dismissed as **laziness, weakness, or just part of the job**. It wasn't until recently that burnout was recognized as a **legitimate medical condition**, not just a vague feeling of being "over it." The World Health

Organization now classifies burnout as an **occupational syndrome**, a condition directly linked to **chronic workplace stress that has not been successfully managed**. But what's alarming is that **burnout is no longer confined to the workplace.** It has seeped into every aspect of modern life, affecting students, parents, caregivers, entrepreneurs—people from all walks of life.

At its core, burnout is different from regular stress. Stress is the body's response to **pressure or demands**, but it comes and goes. Burnout is **stress that never switches off**, leading to **a total depletion of physical, mental, and emotional resources**. While stress makes people feel anxious and overwhelmed, burnout makes them feel **numb, detached, and hopeless**. It's not just the feeling of having too much to do—it's the feeling that nothing matters anymore.

One of the **most dangerous aspects of burnout** is that it doesn't always look the way people expect it to. The **typical image** of burnout is someone **too exhausted to get out of bed, emotionally drained, and unable to function**. And while this is true for many, **there is another form of burnout that goes unnoticed—atypical burnout**. This version doesn't look like exhaustion; it looks like **hyper-productivity, obsession with work, and an inability to unplug**.

Many **high-performers** suffer from **atypical burnout** without realizing it. They **overwork, stay engaged, and keep pushing forward**, telling themselves that their success means they can't possibly be burned out. But the **signs are there—**anxiety, restless nights, sudden mood swings, an inability to relax. Instead of disengaging, they double down, convincing themselves that the solution to their exhaustion is simply **to work harder**. This is why **some of the most "successful" people are** also the most burned out—they mistake their inability to slow down for **dedication** rather than **a warning sign**.

And the warning signs are everywhere.

Burnout doesn't just steal energy—it **rewires the brain**. The **prefrontal cortex**, the part responsible for focus, decision-making, and impulse control, starts to **shrink,** making it harder to think clearly. At the same time, the **amygdala**, the brain's fear and stress center, **grows more reactive**, keeping the body **in a permanent state of tension**. This explains why people suffering from burnout often experience **brain fog, forgetfulness, and an inability to concentrate.** Even simple tasks start to feel overwhelming.

Emotional exhaustion is another **major symptom**. It's not just feeling **tired**—it's feeling completely **drained,** like there is nothing left to give. People in **burnout mode** start withdrawing from others, avoiding social interactions not because they dislike people, but because **they don't have the energy to engage**. They lose interest in things they once loved, struggle with motivation, and often experience **a growing sense of detachment from their work, relationships, and even themselves**.

Physically, **burnout is just as damaging**. Chronic exhaustion **weakens the immune system**, making people **more susceptible to illness**. It **raises inflammation**, increasing the risk of heart disease, digestive issues, and autoimmune conditions. Sleep becomes disrupted—not just from **too little rest, but from poor-quality sleep that doesn't actually restore energy**. This is why people with burnout often wake up feeling just as tired as when they went to bed.

One of the **biggest reasons burnout has exploded into a global epidemic** is the way modern culture **glorifies resilience**. The **hustle mindset** tells people to keep pushing, to **grind harder, sacrifice sleep, and power through**. People wear exhaustion like a **badge of honor**, believing that needing rest is a sign of weakness. But this **toxic resilience culture** is one of the biggest contributors to burnout.

True resilience isn't about **ignoring exhaustion**—it's about **recognizing when to rest and recharge**. The modern obsession with **productivity at all costs** has made people believe that taking breaks is a **luxury**, when in reality, it's a **biological necessity**. A machine that never gets serviced will eventually break down. The human body and mind work the same way.

The **truth about burnout** is that it doesn't discriminate. It affects **young and old, rich and poor, corporate workers and freelancers, parents and students**. It doesn't matter if someone is passionate about their work or not—**anyone can burn out**. And because **burnout builds slowly,** many don't notice it until they are in **full collapse mode**, struggling to function in ways they never have before.

The real danger of burnout is **not just what it does to the present—but what it does to the future.** Burnout isn't just exhaustion—it's **a total depletion of the body's ability to heal, focus, and recover.** Left unchecked, it can take months—or even years—to reverse. The longer it goes on, the harder it is to bounce back.

Recognizing burnout **before it reaches the point of collapse** is critical. The world today pushes people toward exhaustion and then **expects them to self-repair without any real change to the system causing the damage**. Understanding burnout isn't just about **individual survival**—it's about changing the way modern life treats **work, rest, and human well-being**.

Because **if burnout continues at the rate it's spreading**, the real crisis won't just be an exhausted workforce. It will be **an entire generation too depleted to enjoy the very lives they worked so hard to build.**

CHAPTER 3

Your Phone Is Not Just a Tool—It's an Addiction Machine

The moment a person wakes up, their hand instinctively reaches for their phone. Before their second eye is even open, they are scrolling—through emails, through news, through social media updates that flood their screen before their brain has even had a chance to fully wake up. This isn't just a habit. It's a deeply ingrained **neurological loop**, one designed by technology itself.

Most people think of their phone as a **tool**, something they control, something they use when they need it. But the reality is far more complex. A smartphone is not just a **neutral device**—it is an **addiction machine**, engineered to **steal attention, hijack brain chemistry, and keep people glued to their screens for as long as possible**. And the worst part? Most people don't even realize it's happening.

Every time someone **picks up their phone, their brain gets a small hit of dopamine**, the same chemical that reinforces habits, the same neurotransmitter that makes gambling and drug use so addictive. This is not by accident. Tech companies have spent years perfecting **the psychology of compulsion**, designing notifications, scrolling mechanics, and content algorithms that **keep users engaged for as long as possible**. The more time someone spends on their phone, the more data they generate, and the more profit these platforms make.

This is how **Popcorn Brain** begins. The term was first coined by researchers to describe a brain that has been overstimulated by **constant digital input**, making it **restless, impatient, and unable to tolerate boredom**. In the past, waiting in line at a grocery store or sitting in a waiting room meant **staring into space, letting the mind wander, allowing thoughts to flow naturally**. Now, those moments of quiet are almost nonexistent. The second there is a pause, the phone comes out. People no longer give their brains **even a few seconds of stillness**—every gap is filled with an instant dopamine hit, a quick distraction, another digital fix.

And it's happening at an **unbelievable scale**. Studies have shown that the **average person checks their phone 2,617 times a day**. Some **check it even more**. That means **hundreds of unconscious phone grabs**—while eating, while walking, while waiting for an elevator, even while watching TV. The phone has become a **phantom limb**, something people reach for reflexively, whether they need it or not.

The rise of **doomscrolling** has made this problem even worse. During times of global crisis, tragedy, or uncertainty, people instinctively turn to their phones for updates. They **scroll endlessly**, consuming bad news in a cycle that feels impossible to break. This isn't just curiosity—it's a **biological survival mechanism**. The **human brain is wired to seek out threats**, a leftover instinct from an era when **knowing about dangers in the environment could mean the difference between life and death**. But now, this mechanism **works against us**. Instead of keeping people safe, it keeps them trapped in **a loop of stress, fear, and anxiety**, unable to disconnect even when the information is overwhelming.

Social media has only added **another layer** to the addiction. In theory, these platforms are designed to **connect people,** to bring them closer together. In reality, they have done the opposite. The **comparison culture** fueled by social media has made **millions feel more anxious, more insecure, and more alone than ever before**.

Every post, every story, every highlight reel is a **carefully curated illusion**, showing only the best, most polished moments of someone's life. And yet, scrolling through these perfect snapshots, people can't help but **compare their real, unfiltered lives to the artificial perfection on their screens**. It's an **unwinnable game**, one that leaves users feeling **like they are always falling behind, always missing out, never quite enough**. This is why studies have found that **heavy social media use is linked to higher rates of depression, anxiety, and loneliness**. It's not just about the content—it's about the **constant reinforcement of a distorted reality**, one that makes **real life feel dull and inadequate by comparison**.

Perhaps the greatest irony is that despite being **more digitally connected than any generation before**, people are also feeling **more isolated than ever**. The ease of **instant messaging, video calls, and social media** has **replaced face-to-face interactions**, creating a world where people are always in touch but rarely feel truly connected. The rise of loneliness is now being recognized as a **global epidemic**, one with serious **mental and physical health consequences**. In fact, research has shown that **chronic loneliness can be as damaging to health as smoking 15 cigarettes a day.**

What makes **phone addiction so dangerous** is that **it doesn't feel like an addiction**. There's no single moment where someone realizes they've lost control—no dramatic rock bottom, no obvious sign that something has gone wrong. Instead, **it happens slowly, invisibly,** as the minutes spent on a screen stretch into hours, as real-life conversations become less frequent, as attention spans shrink and deep thinking becomes harder.

People tell themselves they can quit anytime, that they are just checking their phone quickly, that it's just part of modern life. But the **truth is much more unsettling**. The very devices that were meant to bring **convenience, efficiency, and connection** have instead become **constant sources of stress, distraction, and exhaustion**.

And the real question is: **If this trend continues, what happens next?**

CHAPTER 4

The Hidden Dangers of a Sedentary Life

The modern world has engineered movement out of everyday life. People wake up and **sit**—to eat breakfast, to commute, to work. Hours pass as bodies remain still, eyes locked on screens, hands barely moving except to type, scroll, or click. By the end of the day, exhaustion sets in, not from exertion, but from the strange paradox of **being completely drained without moving at all**.

It wasn't always this way. For most of human history, life required movement. Walking wasn't a choice; it was how people got from one place to another. Physical labor was an unavoidable part of existence.

Even household chores demanded constant motion. But in the span of just a few generations, everything changed. **Technology replaced effort.** Screens replaced outdoor life. Work shifted from fields and factories to desks and devices. **The result? A world where sitting has quietly become one of the most dangerous things people do every day.**

Researchers now call **sitting the new smoking—a silent, underestimated health crisis** with long-term consequences just as deadly as tobacco use. Studies have linked **prolonged sitting** to **heart disease, obesity, diabetes, and even early death**. But what's even more alarming is the way inactivity **impacts the brain.**

The human body wasn't built to be still for extended periods. Movement isn't just about muscles and joints; it's about **cognition, emotion, and mental clarity.** Every time a person moves, even just by walking, **blood flow increases, delivering oxygen**

and nutrients to the brain. This process helps regulate mood, improve focus, and clear mental fog. But when movement is removed from daily life, **brain function declines in ways that aren't immediately noticeable—but are deeply damaging over time.**

People who sit for long hours **report higher levels of anxiety, depression, and mental fatigue.** Part of this is biological—**a lack of movement disrupts brain chemistry,** leading to **higher cortisol levels, lower serotonin production, and sluggish cognitive processing.** But another factor is more psychological: **sedentary living keeps people trapped inside their heads.** Without movement, stress lingers longer, thoughts loop endlessly, and the physical release that comes from activity **never happens.**

This is why **stress and inactivity feed into each other,** creating a dangerous cycle. Someone under stress is more likely to stay still—whether from exhaustion, lack of motivation, or simply the feeling of being overwhelmed. But the more sedentary they become, the worse their stress gets. **The brain needs movement to process and release tension,** yet modern life ensures that people move less than ever.

This cycle is made worse by another major factor: **stress eating.** When the body is under pressure, the brain craves **high-fat, high-sugar foods**—a survival mechanism leftover from ancient times when **food scarcity meant that any source of quick energy was necessary for survival.** But today, this instinct works against people. Instead of helping them escape danger, it pushes them toward **processed, calorie-dense foods that offer comfort but worsen physical health.** And once poor eating habits take hold, they interfere with **sleep,** which in turn **increases stress and fatigue,** making movement even more difficult.

It's a **self-perpetuating loop: stress leads to inactivity, inactivity fuels poor eating, poor eating disrupts sleep, and lack of sleep increases stress.** The body and brain become trapped in a cycle of exhaustion—one that leaves people feeling drained, foggy, and burned out, even if they haven't physically exerted themselves at all.

The solution, however, is surprisingly simple. **Movement is medicine.** And the best part? **It doesn't have to be extreme.** People assume that fixing this problem requires hours at the gym, but the science shows something far more encouraging: **even a short, 20-minute walk can reset the stress response, clear mental fog, and improve mood.**

When people walk, their bodies release **endorphins**—natural chemicals that act as built-in pain relievers and mood boosters. The simple act of **moving forward**—one foot after the other—signals to the brain that it is not stuck, that it is actively engaging with the world, that it is not trapped in an endless loop of stress. The benefits aren't just mental. **Walking strengthens the heart, improves circulation, lowers blood pressure, and even enhances memory and creativity.**

This is why the most effective stress management strategy isn't **a new diet, a supplement, or a complicated wellness routine**. It's movement. Regular, consistent, and natural movement. Something as small as **standing up and stretching every hour, walking outside instead of scrolling, or taking the stairs instead of the elevator** can make a measurable difference in **brain function and emotional well-being**.

The real danger of a sedentary life isn't just what it does to the body—it's **how it quietly reshapes the mind.** It steals energy, dims cognitive sharpness, and makes **stress feel heavier than it really is**. But the human body wasn't designed for stillness. It was built to move, and every step away from the chair, away from the screen, and back into the physical world is a step toward better mental and physical health.

The question isn't whether movement makes a difference—it's whether people will choose to reclaim it before it's too late.

CHAPTER 5

The Stress Contagion—How It Spreads Without You Noticing

Stress is often thought of as a personal burden—something that exists within the mind, shaped by personal struggles, deadlines, responsibilities, and emotional pressures. But stress doesn't stay contained within individuals. It spreads. Without a single word spoken, without any conscious effort, stress can move from person to person, rippling through workplaces, families, and entire communities like an invisible virus.

It happens in subtle ways. A tense coworker rushes into a meeting, their posture stiff, their breathing shallow. No one in the room says anything, but suddenly, **the air feels heavier**. A parent comes home exhausted, their energy drained from the day. Within minutes, their child, who had been playing happily, becomes irritable. A stranger sighs loudly in a waiting room, and the people nearby—who had been feeling fine—start shifting uncomfortably in their seats, their muscles tensing without them even realizing why.

This isn't just social mimicry. **Stress is biologically contagious.** Researchers have discovered that simply witnessing someone in distress triggers the same stress response in an observer's brain as if they were experiencing the distress themselves. The human nervous system, built for survival, is wired to **detect and absorb** the emotional states of those nearby.

The mechanism behind this is both psychological and physiological. At the heart of it is **mirror neurons**, specialized cells in the brain that allow people to "feel" what others feel. These neurons were originally thought to be responsible for learning through imitation—watching someone smile makes a person more likely to smile back. But the discovery of **stress contagion** suggests that mirror neurons do more than just reflect outward behaviors. They also reflect **internal emotional states**, which means that being around a stressed individual can **cause your body to enter a stressed state—even if nothing is actually happening to you.**

This is why certain environments—**toxic workplaces, chaotic households, even an anxious friend group—can turn stress into an endless cycle.** One person's overwhelm becomes another's. A single moment of tension multiplies, expanding beyond the individual until an entire space feels weighed down by an almost tangible heaviness.

This effect is particularly pronounced in workplaces, where stress is often worn as a badge of honor. People see their overworked colleagues, the late-night emails, the unspoken expectation that being "always on" means being valuable. The pressure builds, and soon, stress becomes not just **accepted** but **expected**. Burnout doesn't happen in isolation—it happens in cultures where stress is both normalized and shared.

In families, the pattern can be even stronger. Children, especially, **absorb stress like sponges**, reacting not just to what their parents say, but to how they carry their stress in their tone, their facial expressions, their pauses between sentences. Even partners who have been together for years start to mirror each other's emotional states, unknowingly syncing their nervous systems in ways that amplify the burden of stress.

This leads to the **Vibe Effect**—the phenomenon where people's bodies react to the energy of those around them before their minds even process it. It explains why certain people feel "draining" while others feel energizing. It's why entering a room where people are arguing—even if they stop when you walk in—still feels suffocating. The **electromagnetic field of the human heart extends up to fifteen feet**, meaning that simply being near someone in distress can cause subtle physiological shifts in your body, increasing **heart rate variability and cortisol levels** before you even realize what's happening.

But just as stress can spread, so can its opposite. **The human nervous system is highly attuned to safety, connection, and regulation.** This is why **some people have a calming effect**—their presence alone seems to slow the pace of a room, making conversations feel smoother, interactions feel less charged, and people feel more at ease.

This is what researchers call **the therapeutic presence**—the ability to create a stabilizing emotional field that others subconsciously respond to. Physicians who cultivate this presence see patients with **better health outcomes**. Leaders who develop it create teams that **thrive under pressure instead of collapsing from stress**. Parents who embody it raise children who are **more emotionally secure, even in uncertain times**.

Developing a therapeutic presence isn't about saying the right words. It's about **embodying emotional steadiness**—through breath, posture, tone, and intention. It means being the one in the room who does **not** take on the collective stress, who does not absorb the anxiety of others, who holds steady even when things feel uncertain.

The key to **breaking the cycle of stress contagion** is not isolation—it's **learning how to stop absorbing stress from others**. This requires **active,**

intentional boundary setting. It means recognizing that **you are not obligated to carry other people's emotional burdens.**

Some simple ways to break the cycle:

- **Visual distancing** – When around highly stressed people, imagine an invisible barrier between you and them. It's a mental trick, but it helps create **emotional separation** so that their stress doesn't invade your state of mind.

- **Controlled breathing** – If you feel someone else's tension seeping into your body, take **slow, deep belly breaths**. This signals to your brain that you are **not in immediate danger**, preventing an unconscious stress response.

- **Limiting exposure to toxic environments** – Some workplaces, relationships, and social circles **run on stress**. If you're surrounded by people who treat stress as normal, it's time to reconsider how much access they have to your energy.

- **Intentional recalibration** – After being in a stressful environment, engage in an activity that **resets your nervous system**: go for a walk, listen to calming music, or engage in deep breathing. Just as people wash their hands after touching something dirty, **emotional residue needs to be rinsed away too.**

- **Becoming the calm in the storm** – Instead of absorbing stress, train yourself to **anchor into a steady, regulated state.** When people are anxious around you, **slow your breathing, lower your tone, and regulate yourself first**. This counteracts stress contagion and creates a **stabilizing effect** on those around you.

The reality is this: **you can't stop stress from existing, but you can stop carrying what isn't yours.** You can't control other people's energy, but you can control how much of it you let in. And the more people who break the cycle, the less power stress contagion has.

Every anxious conversation, every high-pressure environment, every overwhelming social interaction is an opportunity—to **either absorb stress or deflect it**. And in a world that seems to be getting more stressed by the day, the ability to **stand steady in the face of it** is not just a skill. It's a necessity.

CHAPTER 6

The Loneliness Epidemic—The Worst Side Effect of Modern Life

Loneliness is not just an emotion—it's a crisis, a slow-moving epidemic that has embedded itself into modern life. It's a paradox that defies logic: in an age where people are more connected than ever, millions are suffering from an aching sense of isolation. The world has never been more digitally intertwined, yet genuine human connection is slipping further out of reach.

The numbers tell a chilling story. Across the globe, **over 330 million people go at least two weeks without speaking to anyone in person.** For some, it's longer. They live in cities buzzing with activity, yet feel invisible. They scroll through endless feeds, see countless faces, engage in fleeting interactions—but none of it fills the void. In a world that glorifies independence and self-sufficiency, loneliness has become **a silent, unspoken epidemic.**

And the consequences are staggering. **Loneliness is not just an emotional struggle—it is a medical one.** Researchers have found that chronic social isolation increases the risk of heart disease, high blood pressure, depression, and even dementia. The health effects of loneliness are so severe that studies have equated its impact to smoking **15 cigarettes a day**. It weakens the immune system, accelerates cognitive decline, and **shortens life expectancy.** Yet, it remains one of the least discussed public health issues of the modern era.

But what exactly is causing this crisis? It's easy to blame technology. Social media, smartphones, and constant digital interactions have created **the illusion of connection**—a world where messages are sent in seconds, yet meaningful conversations are dwindling. People have become more accustomed to **typing than talking, reacting than engaging, scrolling than listening.**

But the problem runs deeper than screen time. **Cultural shifts have reshaped the way people interact.** Remote work has eliminated daily office interactions. Urbanization has pulled people away from family units. Social norms have made it harder to start conversations with strangers. Even friendships, once built on shared time and experiences, are now being replaced by passive online exchanges—likes, comments, and brief check-ins that lack depth.

And then, there's the **stigma.** Admitting loneliness feels like a confession of failure. Society romanticizes being busy, being independent, being unbothered.

People are afraid to reach out because they assume others are too busy, too preoccupied, too indifferent. And so, the cycle continues—**millions suffer in silence, afraid to admit that what they truly need is connection.**

But loneliness is not just about the absence of people. **It's about the absence of meaningful relationships.** Some people feel deeply connected even with a small circle, while others feel painfully alone in a crowd. The difference lies in **the quality of interactions, not the quantity.**

So how do people break free from this epidemic? The solution is neither instant nor easy. It requires **intentionality**—a shift from passive digital interactions to real-world engagement. It means making **consistent, meaningful efforts** to nurture relationships, instead of assuming that connections will sustain themselves.

Some simple but powerful ways to combat loneliness:

- **Prioritizing real conversations** – Instead of texting, make a call. Instead of a quick "like," leave a meaningful comment or ask a question. **Make interactions count.**

- **Creating shared experiences** – Friendship is built on moments, not messages. Plan meet-ups, join a group, or engage in activities where human connection is central.

- **Lowering the social barrier** – Initiate small talk. Compliment a stranger. Respond to that invitation. **Social skills weaken when not used.** Rebuilding connections starts with small steps.

- **Being vulnerable** – Deep relationships require **openness.** People often wait for others to reach out, to check in, to make the first move. But true connection happens when one person dares to say, **"I've been feeling lonely too."**

- **Detaching from digital validation** – Social media creates the illusion that everyone is surrounded by friends, living exciting lives. The truth is, **what's posted is not reality.** True connection happens offline, in raw, unfiltered moments.

Loneliness does not have to be a life sentence. It is reversible, repairable. But it requires breaking free from the **false comforts of digital interaction** and stepping back into the unpredictable, often awkward, but deeply fulfilling reality of **human connection.**

The antidote to loneliness isn't found in more scrolling, more distractions, or more superficial interactions. It's found in **one meaningful conversation at a time.**

CHAPTER 7

The Burnout Myth—Why Hustle Culture Is Failing Us

Burnout has been glorified, disguised, and rebranded as ambition, dedication, and resilience. Society has embraced **hustle culture**—a relentless, never-stop-moving mentality that treats exhaustion as a badge of honor. The myth is simple but dangerous: **the harder you work, the more successful you'll be.** But beneath this illusion of productivity lies a grim reality—**people are running themselves into the ground, mistaking motion for progress.**

The problem is not just overworking. **It's the belief that pushing through exhaustion is the only path to success.** The idea that if someone isn't constantly grinding, they're falling behind. That if they aren't overwhelmed, they aren't doing enough. But **this mindset is broken.** It is not making people wealthier, smarter, or more fulfilled. It is making them sicker, more anxious, and disconnected from the very success they are chasing.

The Myth of Toxic Resilience

"Keep going. Push harder. Tough it out." These are the mantras of toxic resilience—the belief that true strength means **endurance at all costs.** The reality? **Resilience is not about ignoring exhaustion—it's about recovering from it.** Yet modern work culture has warped the definition, turning resilience into **a demand rather than a tool.**

The rise of burnout is proof. **More than 70% of people report experiencing at least one symptom**

of burnout. That number is not just a reflection of personal struggles—it is a systemic failure. Companies, industries, and even personal ambitions have become structured around the idea that more work equals more success. But what happens when the body and brain refuse to keep up?

The Illusion of Productivity

Busyness is **not** the same as productivity. Many high-achievers mistake **activity for accomplishment,** spending endless hours responding to emails, attending meetings, and juggling multiple tasks, believing they are making progress. In reality, their **cognitive efficiency is declining,** their ability to make good decisions is deteriorating, and their creativity is being stifled.

Studies have shown that **multitasking weakens the prefrontal cortex,** the part of the brain responsible for decision-making, problem-solving, and critical thinking. The constant switching between tasks lowers efficiency and increases mental fatigue. Yet, hustle culture glorifies this behavior—rewarding those who can juggle the most without acknowledging that **true productivity comes from deep focus, not divided attention.**

What's Your Endgame?

It's a question few people stop to ask. **What is all of this for?** Many entrepreneurs, executives, and high-performers push themselves to the brink under the assumption that it will "pay off" someday. But when does "someday" arrive?

Without a clear **endgame**, burnout becomes inevitable. The grind becomes an endless loop, where **success is always just one more late night, one more sacrificed weekend, one more deal away.** But success without sustainability is **self-destruction in disguise.**

The Goldilocks Principle of Stress

Not all stress is bad. Some stress is necessary for **growth, innovation, and achievement.** This is where the Goldilocks Principle comes in—finding the **right** amount of stress. **Too little, and there's no challenge. Too much, and there's collapse.** The key is balance: **enough stress to push forward, but not so much that it leads to breakdown.**

Signs you're in the danger zone:

- You can't unplug—even after work hours.
- You measure your worth by your workload.
- You're constantly exhausted, yet feel like you haven't done enough.
- You sacrifice personal relationships and health for professional goals.
- You feel guilty for resting, as if productivity equals morality.

Mind Over Matter? No—Mind Needs Matter

The brain is not a machine. It is **a biological organ that needs fuel, rest, and recovery.** The idea that success is **purely a mindset** ignores the basic **neuroscience of exhaustion.** Just like muscles need rest after an intense workout, the brain needs downtime to process information, form new ideas, and function optimally.

But modern work culture fights against this reality. Breaks are seen as weakness. Rest is seen as laziness. Time off is seen as lost progress. And yet, science shows that the most successful people are **not those who work the longest, but those who work the smartest.**

Breaking the Burnout Cycle

The antidote to burnout is **not quitting—it's redefining success.**

- **Redefine productivity:** It's about **impact, not hours.** Measure success by what's accomplished, not how long it took.

- **Honor breaks:** Small, intentional pauses throughout the day are **not luxuries—they are necessities.** Even **a 10-second pause resets stress levels.**

- **Learn to unplug: Rest is productive.** The best ideas, the best decisions, and the best work come **after** the brain has had a chance to recharge.

- **Prioritize the long game:** Burnout is a fast sprint to nowhere. True success comes from **sustaining energy, not burning through it.**

The burnout myth has fooled millions into believing that **more work equals more worth.** But the truth is clear: **grind culture is failing us.** Real resilience is not about enduring exhaustion—it's about **learning when to step back, recharge, and come back stronger.**

CHAPTER 8

How to Take Back Control—The Five Resets That Work

Taking back control in the digital age is not about radical changes—it's about **small, consistent resets** that shift the trajectory of daily life. Stress, burnout, and digital overload are not permanent states. They are conditions shaped by habits, choices, and environments, which means they can be reshaped. The key is understanding that transformation **doesn't come from willpower alone**—it comes from creating systems that make **balance the default, not the exception.** These five resets offer a structured way to reclaim mental clarity, emotional resilience, and physical well-being.

Reset 1: Get Clear on What Matters Most

The constant **chase for more**—more productivity, more success, more distractions—has blurred the line between what's urgent and what's truly important. Without clarity, life becomes **a series of reactive decisions rather than intentional choices.** The way forward is the **M.O.S.T. Framework**—a simple yet powerful way to refocus priorities.

- **M – Motivating:** If a goal doesn't spark even the smallest level of excitement, it won't stick.

- **O – Objective:** Goals need to be specific, not vague ideas like "be less stressed." Instead, "take a 15-minute walk at noon" is concrete and achievable.

- **S – Small:** Overhauling life overnight is unrealistic. Small, consistent progress is far more effective than sweeping, unsustainable changes.

- **T – Timely:** Without a timeline, goals get postponed. Time-bound actions drive commitment.

The moment a person starts **setting small, meaningful targets**—rather than vague, overwhelming resolutions—their brain reorients toward progress rather than stress. **Clarity brings back purpose.** And purpose **is the antidote to burnout.**

Reset 2: Build Digital Boundaries

Technology is not inherently harmful—but **its unrestricted presence is.** The endless news cycle, notifications, and social comparisons are not passive; they are **active stress triggers.** Without intentional boundaries, the brain stays **in a perpetual state of hyperstimulation.** Two strategies make an immediate difference:

- **The Media Diet Rule** – Cutting off news consumption altogether is unrealistic. The key is limiting exposure without **falling into ignorance.** The rule is simple: **Consume the news once a day, from a trusted source, for no longer than 20 minutes.**

- **The 10-Foot Rule** – Where the phone is, attention follows. **Keeping the phone at least 10 feet away during focused work or relaxation automatically reduces mindless scrolling.** Out of reach means out of habit. The fewer unnecessary interactions with screens, the more cognitive space remains for **real focus, real presence, real rest.**

Reset 3: Move More, Sit Less

Sitting is **one of the most underestimated stressors on the brain.** When movement stops, **mental sluggishness begins.** The solution isn't an extreme fitness regimen—it's **consistent, strategic movement.**

- **The 20-Minute Movement Fix** – Science has shown that moving the body for **even 20 minutes a day** can lower cortisol levels, improve memory, and restore mental clarity. **A short walk, stretching, or light activity is enough to reset stress chemistry.**

- **The Science of Exercise and Stress Reduction** – Exercise isn't just about physical fitness. It is **one of the most powerful tools for mental resilience.** Movement increases **dopamine, serotonin, and endorphins**—the chemicals that counteract anxiety and exhaustion. **The less the body moves, the more the brain suffers.**

Reset 4: Master Your Breath

Breathing is the one physiological function that can be **both automatic and consciously controlled.**

This means **it's the fastest way to shift the body from stress mode to recovery mode.**

- **Diaphragmatic Breathing** – The stress response speeds up breathing, making it shallow and rapid. **Diaphragmatic breathing (deep belly breathing) is a biological signal** to the nervous system to slow down.
- **Stop, Breathe, Be** – A micro-reset that can be done anywhere, anytime:
  1. Stop what you're doing.
  2. Take a slow inhale through the nose for **four seconds.**
  3. Hold for **four seconds.**
  4. Exhale through the mouth for **six seconds.**
  5. Repeat three times.

The shift is instant. The nervous system **switches from fight-or-flight to calm. One breath at a time, stress loses its grip.**

Reset 5: Reconnect With People

Burnout, digital fatigue, and emotional exhaustion **thrive in isolation.** Human connection is **the most underrated stress reliever.** But in a world where relationships are often reduced to messages and emojis, true connection **must be rebuilt intentionally.**

- **The Power of Real Conversations** – The depth of human connection has deteriorated into **surface-level interactions.** A simple rule: **Have at least one real, unfiltered, uninterrupted conversation each day.** Even **a 5-minute exchange with full attention can be enough to reduce stress and reset emotional well-being.**

- **Therapeutic Writing** – Studies show that **journaling**—especially expressive writing—**releases mental tension, lowers cortisol, and strengthens self-awareness.** Writing is **not** about keeping records—it's about releasing thoughts from the mind to the page.

- **Live a Lifetime in a Day** – Each day should include six essential elements:
    1. **One real conversation** (human connection)
    2. **One moment of movement** (physical reset)
    3. **One break from technology** (digital detox)
    4. **One act of mindfulness** (breathwork, gratitude, or reflection)
    5. **One goal, no matter how small** (progress, not perfection)
    6. **One moment of joy** (laughter, music, or creativity)

Life doesn't happen in months or years. It happens **in moments, in days.** The more these small resets are built into the daily structure, the **less stress and burnout take over.**

CONCLUSION

The digital age has transformed the way we live, work, and connect—but it has also pushed the human brain to **a breaking point.** Stress, burnout, and mental exhaustion are no longer isolated struggles; they have become **a global crisis.** If nothing changes, the toll on mental and physical health will only deepen, leading to **a future where emotional depletion is the norm rather than the exception.**

The Road Ahead: Why This Crisis Will Only Worsen If We Don't Act Now

Technology is advancing **faster than human biology can adapt.** Our brains were never designed to handle **the relentless flood of information, notifications, and demands** that modern life throws at them. The rise of **artificial intelligence, automation, and digital hyper connectivity** will only increase the pressure—unless we take control.

If left unaddressed, stress and burnout will continue to manifest in ways society is **only beginning to understand**—chronic fatigue, cognitive overload, emotional numbness, and a sharp decline in overall well-being. The **mental health crisis will not fix itself.** The modern world rewards those who keep pushing—until they can't anymore. The future will be defined by **those who learn how to reset, not just keep running.**

The Hopeful Side: Why Science, Self-Awareness, and Small Changes Can Reverse the Trend

The same technology that contributes to stress and burnout **can also be part of the solution.** Neuroscience, behavioral psychology, and digital well-being research **have proven that small, intentional changes can reset the brain's balance.** The key is self-awareness—understanding how **daily habits** shape mental health, then making **conscious shifts** toward resilience rather than exhaustion.

The most **promising discovery in stress science** is this: The brain is **highly adaptable.** Even after years of digital overload and burnout, **mental clarity, focus, and emotional stability can be restored.** The process doesn't require extreme transformations—**it requires consistency.** A structured approach to stress management, digital boundaries, movement, mindfulness, and social connection can **reverse** the effects of chronic exhaustion.

How We Can All Be Part of the Solution—Starting Today

This isn't just about individual well-being; **it's about reshaping the way we interact with the world.** Employers, educators, policymakers, and technology leaders must **acknowledge the mental cost of the digital age** and design systems that prioritize **human**

well-being over constant productivity. But the most immediate changes begin on a personal level.

Each person has **the power to break free from stress-driven cycles.** The choice to step away from a screen, to reclaim movement, to reconnect with others, to take a mindful breath—**these are small but revolutionary acts.** The world will continue to demand more, but **you can choose to set boundaries, to rest, to restore.**

Final Words of Encouragement: Your Brain Deserves Better. Your Life Deserves Balance.

This book is not about escaping modern life—it's about learning how to **navigate it with resilience, clarity, and control.** The digital world isn't going anywhere, and stress will always exist. But the difference between **overwhelm and balance** isn't found in external circumstances. **It's found in the way we respond.**

Your brain was never built to be **in a constant state of stress, distraction, and exhaustion.** It deserves **rest, focus, and connection.** Your life was not meant to be **an endless race toward more.** It deserves **depth, purpose, and joy.**

This is not about perfection. It's about **making better choices, one at a time.** Small shifts create momentum. And momentum—when sustained—**transforms everything.**